Pocket Books

Dogs

Kane Miller
A DIVISION OF EDC PUBLISHING

First American Edition 2019
Kane Miller, A Division of EDC Publishing

Copyright © Green Android Ltd 2018

For information contact:
Kane Miller, A Division of EDC Publishing
P.O. Box 470663
Tulsa, OK 74147-0663
www.kanemiller.com
www.edcpub.com
www.usbornebooksandmore.com

Please note that every effort has been made to check the accuracy of
the information contained in this book, and to credit the copyright
holders correctly. Green Android Ltd apologize for any unintentional
errors or omissions, and would be happy to include revisions to content
and/or acknowledgements in subsequent editions of this book.

Printed and bound in China, July 2020
ISBN. 978-1-61067-878-0 Library of Congress Control Number: 2018942404

Images © Shutterstock.com: Bull terrier © Alexandra Morrison Photo, Chinese Shar Pei © Alexeysun,
Keeshound, West Highland Terrier © anetapics, Rhodesian Ridgeback © Anke van Wyk, standard poodle ©
Anna K Majer, German shorthaired pointer © Baevskiy Dmitry, Pomeranian © barinovalen, Hungarian
Komondo © Bea Kis, great dane © belu gheorghe, Belgian Malinois Shepherd © BIGANDT.COM, Parson
Russell Terrier © Bildagentur Zoonar GmbH, portuguese water dog © Brook Robinson, Rottweiler © By Idea
Studio, Brittany Spaniel, Dachshund, Hungarian Vizsla, Irish Terrier, labrador retriever, Petit Basset Griffon
Vendeen, Scottish Terrier © Capture Light, Shih tzu © chaoss, German Shepherd Dog © Christian Mueller,
Boston Terrier © Connie Wade, Staffordshire bull terrier © Couperfield, basset hound, miniature american
shepherd, newfoundland © cynoclub, Cavalier King Charles spaniel © dean bertoncelj, Chihuahua © Dennis
Jacobsen, Beagle playing in water, French Bulldog © Dezy, English Setter, havanese © Dorottya Mathe,
Doberman Pinscher, Ibizan Hound, irish wolfhound © DragoNika, German wirehaired pointer © eAlis,
Bearded collie, Japanese Chin, Weimaraner (title page) © Eric Isselee, Pug © evastudio, Cairn Terrier,
Coonhound © everydoghasastory, bichon fries © f8grapher, siberian husky © gillmar, Basenji, Dalmatian,
English bulldog, Giant schnauzer, Greyhound, Pembroke welsh corgi, saint Bernard, Whippet © Grigorita Ko,
Alaskan Malamute, German Shepherd © Grisha Bruev, great pyrenees © HelloRF Zcool, Tibetan Spaniel ©
IMANDRA, Briard Do © JanVlcek, airedale terrier © jarobike, Weimaraner © Jeffery L Willis, Afghan hound
© Jerzy, Search and rescue © Jim Parkin, Leonberger © Julia Siomuha, welsh corgi cardigan © Kachalkina
Veronika, Borzoi © Kim Christensen, grey wolf © Kjetil Kolbjornsrud, Australian shepherd © Ksenia Raykova,
Border Terrier © l i g h t p o e t, cocker spaniel © Labrador Photo Video, bernese mountain dog, bloodhound,
german boxer © Lenkada american bulldog © Little Moon, goldendoodle © Lopol, Tibetan terrier ©
manfredxy, spinone italiano © MarinaGreen, Cockapoo © Martin Christopher Parker, golden retriever ©
Martin Valigursky, Saluki © Natalia Fedosov, Bedlington Terrier © Natalia V Guseva, toy poodle © Nikolai
Tsvetkov, Miniature Schnauzer © OlgaOvcharenko, Miniature schnauzer © olgaru79, German Shepherd ©
Peter Kunasz, Maltese © Photobort, Bullmastiff © photosounds, beagle, italian greyhound, standard
schnauzer © Plotitsyna NiNa, Irish Setter © Reddogs, Mastiff © Ricantimages, Chesapeake Bay Retriever ©
rokopix, Toy fox terrier © Rosa Jay, Norwegian Buhund © Ruben Lopez, Fox-terrier © Sann von Mai, Grand
Basset Griffon Vendeen © Sanne vd Berg Fotografie, hungarian puli © SasaStoc, Akita-inu © Sbolotova,
Yorkshire Terrier © Sergey Lavrentev, Belgian shepherd Tervuren © Serova_Ekaterin, Otterhound ©
sirtravelalot, Samoyed © Stanimir G.Stoev, American Eskimo Dog © Stephaniellen, english springer spaniel ©
StockPhotosLV, Lhasa-apso © SubertT, old english sheepdog , Rough collie, shetland sheepdog © Svetlana
Valoueva, Bouvier des Flandres © Tatyana Kuznetsova, Xoloitzcuintli © TatyanaPanova, miniature poodle ©
TeodorLazarev, Norwegian Elkhound © Tiina Tuomaala, Shiba Inu © TOM KAROL, wheaten terrier © Vadim
Petrako, Border Collie © Vera Zinkova, Chow Chow, Miniature Pinscher Dog © Vkarlov, Pekingese ©
VladFotoMag, Papillon, Schipperke © volofin, Wire Fox Terrier © Waldemar Dabrowski, toy manchester
terrier © WileeCole Photography, labradoodle © zstock, Chinese Crested Dog © Zuzule.

Introducing dogs

Fifteen thousand years ago, our ancestors domesticated gray wolf cubs. Where once these wild canines, *Canis lupis*, hunted prey to feed the pack, they now became companions and helped humankind hunt food to feed the village. Modern dogs evolved from these wolves and are 98% genetically identical. Years of selective breeding has resulted in around 330 different breeds of dogs.

All dog breeds are believed to be descended from the gray wolf.

Dogs are pack animals that enjoy doing things cooperatively.

Dogs are often used by emergency services for their acute senses.

Characteristics of dogs

Dogs are social animals with an innate pack mentality. Most pet dogs look to their human families – and any other pets in the household – to be their pack.

Dogs have sharp and acute senses. Their hearing can detect sounds that are too high-pitched for human ears. Their eyes, positioned toward the sides of their head, provide a wide field of vision. Dogs can use their sense of smell – some have 300 million receptors to humans' six million – to track scents, which is why they are used as search-and-rescue (SAR) dogs.

How to use this book

This book gives you the essential facts and information on 118 incredible, clever and charming canine breeds.

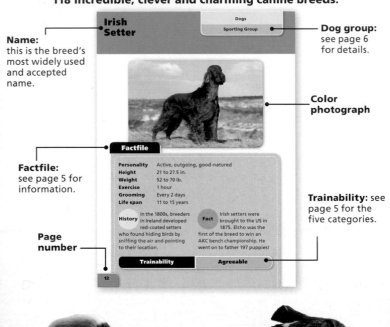

Name: this is the breed's most widely used and accepted name.

Factfile: see page 5 for information.

Page number

Dog group: see page 6 for details.

Color photograph

Trainability: see page 5 for the five categories.

Irish Setter

Dogs
Sporting Group

Factfile

Personality	Active, outgoing, good-natured
Height	21 to 27.5 in.
Weight	52 to 70 lb.
Exercise	1 hour
Grooming	Every 2 days
Life span	11 to 15 years

History In the 1800s, breeders in Ireland developed red-coated setters who found hiding birds by sniffing the air and pointing to their location.

Fact Irish setters were brought to the US in 1875. Elcho was the first of the breed to win an AKC bench championship. He went on to father 197 puppies!

Trainability   **Agreeable**

12

A beagle in pursuit ...

4

Factfile

The Factfiles provide key facts and figures about each dog breed, including typical size and exercise needs.

Personality
A general description of a breed's temperament and intelligence.

Height
Measured in inches (in.) from the ground to the ridge between the shoulder blades (withers). Height of an adult dog is given as a range, average (av.), minimum (min.) or maximum (max.).

Weight
The weight of an adult dog, expressed in pounds (lb.) as a range, average (av.), minimum (min.) or maximum (max.).

Exercise
The ideal amount of exercise the breed needs every day in order to stay healthy.

Grooming
How often the coat needs to be brushed.

Life span
Average life of the breed.

History Information about the breed's forebears, origins, native home and jobs.

Fact Distinguishing features, natural and trained abilities and famous dogs of the breed.

Trainability

These five categories offer insight into how each breed responds to training.

Eager to please

Obedient and easily taught, eager to learn and play.

Easy to train

Sensible and good-natured, training should start early and be consistent.

Agreeable

Well-mannered, but obedience training essential.

Independent

Smart and self-reliant, early socialization recommended.

Stubborn

Very loyal, but can be difficult to train.

Dog groups

In this book, each breed is allocated to one of eight groups. These groups are also used by many canine clubs and organizations.

Sporting dogs

Also known as gun dogs or bird dogs, these dogs are bred (and often trained) to find and retrieve game. They work in cooperation with human partners rather than with a pack of dogs. They are active dogs and make great pets, forming strong bonds with humans.

Working dogs

Strong and intelligent, these dogs' breeding and training prepares them to be guard, military or police dogs, as well as farm or rescue dogs. Often workers first and pets second, they enjoy having a job to do, and regular exercise.

German shepherd guard dog at work.

Toy dogs

Breeds in the toy group are characterized by their small size. Mostly companion or lap dogs, some were bred as miniature versions of an existing breed; others are naturally small. The exercise needs of these dogs vary from breed to breed.

Herding dogs

Often seen working on farms, herding dogs mind sheep, cattle, fowl, pigs and even reindeer! They are active, intelligent dogs, built for an outdoor life. Many have an insulated weatherproof coat. These dogs need vigorous exercise and stimulation.

Hounds

Dogs in this group are bred for scent and sight hunting. Some, like beagles, will track prey over long distances. Others, like greyhounds, have incredible speed. Whether hunting companions or not, hounds make great pets.

Terriers

These highly popular dogs are known for being feisty and energetic, with tons of personality. Terriers were initially bred to hunt and kill vermin and guard the family home and farm. They will chase their prey above ground and below. They are fearless, and even the smaller members of this group, like cairn terriers and Scottish terriers, will take on much larger foes!

A West Highland white terrier ready to play!

Contents

Non-sporting dogs

The dogs in this group vary widely in terms of size, ability and appearance. They were bred for functions beyond hunting and working. Non-sporting dogs include poodles, Dalmations and the Mexican hairless Xoloitzcuintli.

Crossbreeds

This group contains breeds that have only appeared in the last few decades. Sometimes called "designer dogs," these purposely bred mixes are created when two or more breeds are crossed for specific traits.

German Wirehaired Pointer

Factfile

Personality	Affectionate, eager, enthusiastic
Height	22 to 24 in.
Weight	50 to 70 lb.
Exercise	At least 2 hours
Grooming	Weekly
Life span	14 to 16 years

History Crossbreeding of several types of hunting dogs in the late 1800s yielded this all-around gun dog. Well-muscled and determined, it can flush, point and retrieve.

Fact A wiry, weatherproof coat offers protection from brambles and burrs. The beard, dark-brown nose, floppy ears, high-set tail and webbed feet are distinctive and appealing.

Trainability   **Eager to please**

German Shorthaired Pointer

Factfile

Personality	Friendly, smart, biddable, loyal
Height	21 to 25 in.
Weight	45 to 70 lb.
Exercise	At least 2 hours
Grooming	Weekly
Life span	10 to 12 years

History Speed and endurance, a keen nose for pointing, a soft mouth for retrieving and noble looks all come from a wide range of forebears.

Fact Equally happy and adept on land and in water, the German shorthaired pointer will enthusiastically fetch game or sticks or balls – whatever is required.

Trainability | **Agreeable**

Brittany

Factfile

Personality	Bright, fun loving, sensitive
Height	18 to 20.5 in.
Weight	30 to 40 lb.
Exercise	At least 2 hours
Grooming	2 to 3 times a week
Life span	10 to 14 years

History Highly energetic, the Brittany was first bred from French spaniels and English setters and pointers in France in the 1700s to point and retrieve small birds.

Fact Dog team sports such as flyball, as well as agility and field events, are ideal outlets for the medium-sized, short-backed Brittany.

Trainability	Agreeable

English Setter

Factfile

Personality	Friendly, easygoing, bright
Height	24 to 27 in.
Weight	45 to 80 lb.
Exercise	At least 2 hours
Grooming	3 to 4 times a week
Life span	11 to 12 years

History A part of hunting life since the 1300s, they "set" when locating a bird, crouching motionless and raising a paw to indicate the bird's position.

Fact Elegant, with a long, silky and feathered coat and scimitar-shaped tail, the English setter is also fast, with powerfully strong hind legs.

Trainability	Easy to train

Irish Setter

Factfile

Personality	Active, outgoing, good-natured
Height	21 to 27.5 in.
Weight	52 to 70 lb.
Exercise	1 hour
Grooming	Every 2 days
Life span	11 to 15 years

History In the 1800s, breeders in Ireland developed red-coated setters who found hiding birds by sniffing the air and pointing to their location.

Fact Irish setters were brought to the US in 1875. Elcho was the first of the breed to win an AKC bench championship. He went on to father 197 puppies!

Trainability	Agreeable

Spinone Italiano

Factfile

Personality	Sociable, patient, docile
Height	22 to 28 in.
Weight	63 to 86 lb.
Exercise	Long-distance walk daily
Grooming	Weekly
Life span	10 to 12 years

History As portrayed in 15th century Italian art, this hunter located birds in thorny "spinos" bushes by scent, then ambushed them.

Fact Bushy eyebrows, moustache and beard give this dog a gruff look, but along with a wiry coat, help protect its body while hunting.

Trainability	Independent

Hungarian Vizsla

Factfile

Personality	Affectionate, gentle, energetic
Height	21 to 25 in.
Weight	44 to 66 lb.
Exercise	2 hours, walk and run
Grooming	Weekly
Life span	12 to 14 years

History Its forebears may have been the Transylvanian hound and the Turkish yellow dog (extinct), but despite its colorful origins, the breed was scarce until recently.

Fact The vizsla was used to deliver messages during WW I and WW II. Today, even with its willful streak, they are used as therapy and guide dogs.

Trainability   **Eager to please**

Golden Retriever

Factfile

Personality	Friendly, intelligent, devoted
Height	20 to 24 in.
Weight	59 to 75 lb.
Exercise	At least 2 hours
Grooming	Brush 1 to 2 times a week
Life span	10 to 12 years

History A cross between a wavy-coated retriever and the Tweed water spaniel (extinct), the golden retriever first appeared in the 1800s and remains popular.

Fact A calm and social nature combines with a keen sense of smell, great tracking ability and willingness to learn, to make goldens ideal SAR dogs.

Trainability Eager to please

Chesapeake Bay Retriever

Factfile

Personality	Affectionate, bright, sensitive, calm
Height	21 to 26 in.
Weight	55 to 80 lb.
Exercise	Energetic 60 minutes, plus games
Grooming	At least once a week
Life span	10 to 13 years

History This strong swimmer was developed from lesser Newfoundland water dogs and gun dogs, as well as retrievers, to retrieve ducks from the Chesapeake Bay.

Fact The thick, oily and wavy double coat is waterproof and insulating, and the tail acts as a rudder in the water.

Trainability	Agreeable

Labrador Retriever

Factfile

Personality	Friendly, active, outgoing
Height	21 to 25 in.
Weight	55 to 80 lb.
Exercise	45 to 90 minutes, run, walk and games
Grooming	Brush 1 to 2 times a week
Life span	10 to 14 years

History This dog's heritage comes from the water dogs of Newfoundland, Canada, who retrieved ducks from under ice, and fish that had fallen off the hook.

Fact Built to swim with a dense, oily coat, webbed paws and an otter-like tail, Labs come in three coat colors: black, yellow and chocolate.

Trainability   **Eager to please**

17

Cocker Spaniel

Factfile

Personality	Gentle, smart, happy, sensitive
Height	14 to 17 in.
Weight	26 to 35 lb.
Exercise	1 to 2 hours
Grooming	Daily
Life span	12 to 16 years

History Named for the woodcock it flushed from bushes or water, the first cocker spaniel in the US may have arrived on the *Mayflower* in 1620.

Fact The coat can be black, particolor (white plus one or two solid colors) or any solid color other than black (ASCOB). Today, they are mostly show or family dogs.

Trainability   Stubborn

English Springer Spaniel

Factfile

Personality	Friendly, playful, loyal, intelligent
Height	19 to 20 in.
Weight	40 to 55 lb.
Exercise	At least 2 hours
Grooming	3 times a week
Life span	12 to 14 years

History Originally, the springer would flush game birds from tall grasses for the hunter to shoot. A hawk would then retrieve the birds for the hunter.

Fact Springers are used by law enforcement to detect all sorts of things, from drugs and explosives to cell phones and blood.

Trainability	Easy to train

Weimaraner

Factfile

Personality	Friendly, fearless, obedient, intelligent
Height	22 to 27 in.
Weight	50 to 85 lb.
Exercise	At least 2 hours
Grooming	Weekly
Life span	10 to 15 years

History Bloodhounds crossed with hunting dogs bred this aristocratic dog, able to hunt down boar and deer for German nobility in the 1800s.

Fact Nicknamed the "gray ghost" for its short, metallic-like silver-gray coat, this dog has striking looks and build. A dark stripe may run along its back.

Trainability	Independent

Komondor

Factfile

Personality	Loyal, dignified, brave
Height	29.5 in. av.
Weight	80 to 135 lb.
Exercise	2 to 3 short walks
Grooming	Don't brush; separate cords as needed
Life span	10 to 12 years

History This ancient livestock-guarding breed comes from Hungary. Its protective instinct is strong and may turn to aggression—it has a loud bark!

Fact After two years, the fuzzy, curly coat starts to form dreadlock-like cords. To avoid matting, the cords must be separated and trimmed about twice a year.

Trainability	Independent

Standard Schnauzer

Factfile

Personality	Fearless, smart, spirited
Height	17 to 20 in.
Weight	30 to 45 lb.
Exercise	Brisk 60-minute walk
Grooming	Coat, 2 to 3 times a week; beard daily
Life span	13 to 16 years

History In the 1850s, a native German farm dog was crossed with a wolfspitz and a German poodle to create the textured salt-and-pepper coat.

Fact The bristly, distinctive snout ("schnauze" in German) was protection from vermin bites – the schnauzer's target when hunting on the farm.

Trainability	Independent

Giant Schnauzer

Factfile

Personality	Loyal, alert, energetic, intelligent
Height	23.5 to 27.5 ins.
Weight	55 to 80 lb.
Exercise	At least 60-minute brisk walk and play
Grooming	At least 3 times a week
Life span	12 to 15 years

History The giant is a different breed than other schnauzers, and is a cross between a Great Dane, a Bouvier des Flandres and the standard schnauzer.

Fact Originally used to drive cattle, this large and agile dog is still best known as a working dog. Many law enforcement agencies use giant schnauzers.

Trainability	Easy to train

Bernese Mountain Dog

Factfile

Personality	Good-natured, calm, strong
Height	23 to 27.5 in.
Weight	80 to 110 lb.
Exercise	Vigorous 30 to 90 minutes
Grooming	3 times a week, daily when shedding
Life span	6 to 8 years

History Swiss native farm dogs were bred with mastiffs brought in by invading Romans to create these gentle giants. They were almost extinct by the 1890s.

Fact The strong Bernese can haul up to 1,000 pounds – there are cart-pulling competitions! Affable and placid, they are also used as therapy dogs.

Trainability	**Easy to train**

Boxer

Factfile

Personality	Bright, fun loving, active, wary
Height	21 to 25 in.
Weight	55 to 70 lb.
Exercise	At least 1 hour
Grooming	Weekly
Life span	10 to 12 years

History An English bulldog and bullenbeisser (extinct) cross resulted in this strong hunting dog, which uses its undershot jaw to lock on to and hold down prey.

Fact That boxers slobber and snore is well known, but a boxer also holds the world record for the longest tongue – 17 inches!

Trainability	Easy to train

Bullmastiff

Factfile

Personality	Affectionate, loyal, brave, protective
Height	24 to 27 in.
Weight	100 to 130 lb.
Exercise	Gentle 1 to 2 hours
Grooming	1 to 2 times a week
Life span	8 to 10 years

History They crossed two English dogs – a bulldog and a mastiff – and game wardens got a dog that could track a poacher, knock him down and hold him.

Fact A bullmastiff is docile and gentle, but like other dogs will react if its owner needs protection. Though a big dog, a small backyard is all it requires.

Trainability   **Stubborn**

Great Dane

Factfile

Personality	Friendly, patient, dependable
Height	28 to 34 in.
Weight	100 to 200 lb.
Exercise	2 hours
Grooming	Weekly
Life span	7 to 10 years

History This ancient, large dog is from Germany not Denmark. It was used to hunt boar and was the preferred (and pampered) protection dog of the nobility.

Fact Known as a large lap dog, Great Danes are affectionate, love to lean against their owner's legs, and will curl up on a lap given half a chance!

Trainability	**Agreeable**

Mastiff

Factfile

Personality	Courageous, dignified, good-natured
Height	27.5 in. min.
Weight	120 to 230 lb.
Exercise	20 to 30 minutes, twice a day
Grooming	Weekly; daily when shedding
Life span	6 to 10 years

History During the Middle Ages, mastiffs were sometimes suited up in armor and spiked collars to enter a battle. They were also used to guard castles.

Fact A mastiff named Zorba was once the world's largest dog. In 1989 he was 37 inches tall at the withers, 99 inches long and weighed 343 pounds!

Trainability	Agreeable

Newfoundland

Factfile

Personality	Sweet, patient, devoted
Height	27 in. av.
Weight	100 to 150 lb.
Exercise	60-minute walk or swim
Grooming	Weekly
Life span	8 to 10 years

History This breed's ancestor may be the Pyrenees mountain dogs that sailed to Newfoundland, Canada, with fishermen. They became popular ships' dogs.

Fact Large webbed paws make for a strong swimmer! A Newfoundland is said to have rescued Napoleon Bonaparte when he fell overboard.

Trainability	Easy to train

29

Great Pyrenees

Factfile

Personality	Smart, patient, calm
Height	22 to 28 in.
Weight	83 to 110 lb.
Exercise	30 to 45 minutes, less in hot weather
Grooming	Weekly
Life span	10 to 12 years

History This breed evolved from white mountain dogs that guarded livestock. They appeared in Europe 5,000 years ago. In France, they are called "royal dogs."

Fact In the mountains of southern Europe, Pyrenees protected the sheep from wolves and hauled artillery during WW II.

Trainability   **Independent**

Rottweiler

Factfile

Personality	Loyal, intelligent, protective, wary
Height	22 to 27 in.
Weight	85 to 130 lb.
Exercise	At least 2 hours
Grooming	Weekly
Life span	8 to 10 years

History This ancient breed herded and guarded the livestock of the Roman army. It is named for Rottweil, Germany, where a breed-saving program started.

Fact Recognized by its muscled body under a black-and-tan coat, rottweilers need early training and socialization, and enjoy agility and carting activities.

Trainability	Independent

31

Saint Bernard

Factfile

Personality   Playful, charming, inquisitive, calm
Height   26 to 30 in.
Weight   120 to 180 lb.
Exercise   1 hour
Grooming   2 to 3 times a week
Life span   8 to 10 years

History   The Saint Bernard's ability to smell, track and find people lost in snow was recorded in the 1700s by workers at a hospice in Switzerland.

Fact   Beethoven may be a movie-star St. Bernard, but Barry was a real hero. He rescued 40 people – carrying one on his back – between 1800 and 1812.

Trainability	Agreeable

Leonberger

Factfile

Personality	Friendly, gentle, playful
Height	25.5 to 31.5 in.
Weight	90 to 170 lbs.
Exercise	At least 2 hours
Grooming	Twice a week
Life span	8 to 10 years

History First bred in Germany in the 1840s, the leonberger is thought to be a Newfoundland, Saint Bernard, and later Pyrenees, cross.

Fact With its lionlike head (a reference to the crest of its home city, Leonberg), the breed has been royal pet to emperors, kings and tsars.

Trainability	Eager to please

Akita

Factfile

Personality	Courageous, dignified, loyal
Height	24 to 28 in.
Weight	70 to 130 lb.
Exercise	1 hour
Grooming	Weekly
Life span	10 to 12 years

History Originating in a mountainous region of Japan, Akitas were fighting dogs, trained to hunt large animals and herd fish into nets.

Fact The Akita Hachiko walked with his owner to and from the train station every day – then on his own, for nine years after his owner's death.

Trainability	**Independent**

Samoyed

Factfile

Personality	Adaptable, friendly, gentle
Height	19 to 23.5 in.
Weight	35 to 65 lb.
Exercise	At least 1 hour
Grooming	2 to 3 times a week
Life span	12 to 14 years

History Raised by Samoyedic peoples of Siberia to hunt, haul sleds and herd reindeer, Samoyeds also frequently guarded the children of the families they served.

Fact The Samoyed's thick, white coat is well loved, as is its "smiley" grin, formed by the upward-curved corners of its black-lipped mouth.

Trainability	Agreeable

Siberian Husky

Factfile

Personality	Loyal, outgoing, mischievous
Height	20 to 23.5 in.
Weight	35 to 60 lb.
Exercise	At least 2 hours
Grooming	Weekly
Life span	12 to 14 years

History The breed's history can be traced back 2,000 years to the sled dogs of the Siberian Chukchi people, who would haul sleds over vast distances on little food.

Fact The Alaskan Iditarod, a 1,049-mile sled dog race, is often held in sub-zero blizzard conditions. Siberian huskies are used in many of the dog sled teams.

Trainability	Independent

Alaskan Malamute

Factfile

Personality	Affectionate, loyal, playful
Height	22 to 26 in.
Weight	75 to 94 lb.
Exercise	At least 2 hours
Grooming	Weekly
Life span	10 to 14 years

History Originating in Russia 2,000 to 3,000 years ago, the Alaskan Mahlemut people treated this hunting and sled-pulling dog as a member of the family.

Fact Though their jobs have ranged from sniffing out mines to search-and-rescue missions, malamutes are too friendly with people to make useful guard dogs.

Trainability Stubborn

Doberman

Factfile

Personality	Loyal, fearless, alert, wary
Height	24 to 28 in.
Weight	65 to 85 lb.
Exercise	At least 1 hour, plus all-day yard space
Grooming	Weekly
Life span	10 to 12 years

History Terrier, greyhound, Great Dane, pinscher and other breeds were crossed in the 1800s to create the Doberman, a companion and protector dog.

Fact Intelligence, quick reactions, scenting ability, strength and all-around soundness are the breed qualities that make them ideal guard dogs.

Trainability   **Eager to please**

Portuguese Water Dog

Factfile

Personality	Affectionate, adventurous, athletic
Height	17 to 23 in.
Weight	35 to 60 lb.
Exercise	Vigorous 30 to 60 minutes
Grooming	2 to 3 times a week
Life span	11 to 15 years

History In 1297 a monk wrote about a Portuguese water dog rescuing a drowning sailor. Strong swimmers, they would herd fish and retrieve fishing nets.

Fact In 2008 President Barack Obama and his family named their "first dog," a Portuguese, Bo, after musician Bo Diddley.

Trainability	**Easy to train**

Papillon

Factfile

Personality	Friendly, alert, happy
Height	8 to 11 in.
Weight	7 to 10 lb.
Exercise	30 minutes
Grooming	2 to 3 times a week
Life span	12 to 16 years

History One of the oldest toy breeds, the papillon's forebear is the floppy-eared miniature spaniel, but the erect ears may be due to crossing with spitz-type dogs.

Fact The name, French for "butterfly," refers to the fringed, winglike ears. Marie Antoinette held her papillon in her arms when she was led to the guillotine.

Trainability	**Eager to please**

Pomeranian

Factfile

Personality	Inquisitive, bold, lively
Height	6 to 12 in.
Weight	3 to 7 lb.
Exercise	30 minutes
Grooming	3 to 4 times a week
Life span	12 to 16 years

History A spitz breed, like the Samoyeds and malamutes, they weighed 30 pounds and pulled sleds until the 1800s, when breeders began to favor smaller Poms.

Fact Pomeranians keep good company! Mozart dedicated an aria to his dog, Queen Victoria had 35, and Michelangelo's Pom watched as his master painted.

Trainability	Agreeable

Italian Greyhound

Factfile

Personality	Playful, alert, sensitive, athletic
Height	13 to 15 in.
Weight	6 to 15 lb.
Exercise	At least 1 hour
Grooming	Weekly
Life span	12 to 15 years

History Skeletons date the breed back 2,000 years. It survived unchanged until breeders, wanting even smaller dogs, almost destroyed the breed.

Fact They may have once hunted small game – they can run at 25 mph – but are now mostly pets. They are prone to injuries because of "big dog" behavior.

Trainability   **Stubborn**

42

Toy Fox Terrier

Factfile

Personality	Friendly, alert, intelligent, confident
Height	8.5 to 11.5 in.
Weight	3 to 7 lb.
Exercise	15 to 30 minutes, plus yard play
Grooming	Weekly
Life span	13 to 15 years

History These toys were first bred in the 1930s, when fox terriers were crossed with Italian greyhounds, Manchester terriers, Chihuahuas and miniature pinschers.

Fact With confidence and personality aplenty, this small American-bred dog with hunting instincts will have its nose in every nook and cranny.

Trainability	Eager to please

Toy Manchester Terrier

Factfile

Personality	Agile, spirited, intelligent
Height	8 to 13 in.
Weight	12 lb. max.
Exercise	30 minutes
Grooming	Weekly
Life span	14 to 16 years

History The "gentleman's terrier" was developed from the standard Manchester terrier. The toy is smaller, with ears that are wide based and erect.

Fact A clever and watchful dog that loves to be around people, they should be walked on a leash or exercised in a secure, fenced yard – one that is dig proof!

Trainability	Independent

44

Yorkshire Terrier

Factfile

Personality	Affectionate, spirited, intelligent
Height	6 to 9 in.
Weight	4 to 10 lb.
Exercise	30 minutes
Grooming	Daily
Life span	12 to 15 years

History Clydesdale, Paisley, Skye and English terriers were used to breed the Yorkie, which was taken into UK mines and mill houses to control the rats.

Fact If allowed, these tiny dogs will pick fights with much larger dogs. The smallest Yorkie ever recorded was 2.5 inches tall and weighed only 4 ounces.

Trainability

Miniature Pinscher

Factfile

Personality	Fearless, fun loving, proud
Height	10 to 12.5 in.
Weight	8 to 10 lb.
Exercise	30 minutes
Grooming	2 to 3 times a week
Life span	12 to 16 years

History Known as the "king of toys," the min pin was bred in Germany as a ratter. It is probably a mix of terrier, Dachshund and Italian greyhound.

Fact The min pin looks like a small Doberman, but is a different breed. This muscly, square-standing dog has energy to burn, so training must start early.

Trainability   **Independent**

Chihuahua

Factfile

Personality	Charming, graceful, sassy
Height	6 to 9 in.
Weight	2 to 6 lb.
Exercise	At least 30 minutes
Grooming	At least once a week
Life span	14 to 18 years

History This Mexican dog may be a descendant of the Techichi, an ancient South American breed, possibly crossed with the hairless Chinese crested dog.

Fact Chihuahuas come in both short and long coats, and in lots of solid, bi- or tricolors. It can be a loving but timid and nervous companion.

Trainability	**Easy to train**

Chinese Crested

Factfile

Personality	Affectionate, alert, lively
Height	11 to 13 in.
Weight	8 to 12 lb.
Exercise	1 hour
Grooming	Weekly (hairless and coated)
Life span	13 to 18 years

History The breed's origins aren't clear, but it may have come from Africa where it was used as a bed warmer. Chinese sailors then carried it as a ratter.

Fact Cresteds can be hairless (hair on head, tail and feet) or have a long coat (a powder puff). Members of the breed have won multiple ugly dog contests.

Trainability	Agreeable

Japanese Chin

Factfile

Personality	Charming, noble, loving
Height	8 to 11 in.
Weight	4 to 15 lb.
Exercise	30 minutes
Grooming	Twice a week
Life span	10 to 15 years

History The chin originated in China and is related to the Pekingese. Once brought to Japan, it became a royal favorite and was often on display.

Fact Popular and revered in Japan, the chin is immortalized on pottery and in decorations. It arrived in Europe in 1853 – Queen Victoria owned two!

Trainability   **Independent**

49

Maltese

Factfile

Personality	Gentle, playful, charming
Height	8 to 10 in.
Weight	3 to 8 lb.
Exercise	30 minutes, twice a day
Grooming	Daily
Life span	12 to 15 years

History An ancient breed from the island of Malta, its likely ancestors were spitz-type dogs or Tibetan terriers. Trade spread the Maltese into Europe.

Fact The original name for the breed was Roman ladies' dog. In ancient Egypt it was believed that the Maltese had mystical powers of healing.

Trainability	**Agreeable**

Toy Poodle

Factfile

Personality	Agile, intelligent, confident
Height	10 in. max.
Weight	6 to 9 lb.
Exercise	Vigorous 30 minutes, plus games
Grooming	Daily
Life span	10 to 18 years

History The toy poodle was bred down from the standard poodle in the 1700s. Its curly coat grows throughout its life and left untended would form cords.

Fact Its German name, pudel, means "splash about" and refers to its retrieving game birds from water. It is a working dog, not just a fashionable companion.

Trainability	**Eager to please**

Shih Tzu

Factfile

Personality	Affectionate, playful, outgoing
Height	9 to 10.5 in.
Weight	9 to 16 lb.
Exercise	20 minutes, twice a day
Grooming	Daily
Life span	10 to 18 years

History Bred for Chinese emperors and given the name "lion dog," this imperial breed's ancient ancestors were most likely wild kitchen midden dogs.

Fact Famous fans of the shih tzu include Nicole Richie, Mariah Carey, Beyoncé, Colin Farrell, Bill Gates, Queen Elizabeth II and even the Dalai Lama!

Trainability	Agreeable

Cavalier King Charles Spaniel

Factfile

Personality	Doting, gentle, graceful
Height	12 to 13 in.
Weight	12 to 18 lb.
Exercise	Up to 1 hour
Grooming	2 to 3 times a week
Life span	10 to 15 years

History Prized as both a lap dog and sporting dog in 1700s and 1800s UK, the breed was named for King Charles II, the Cavalier King.

Fact A different breed than the King Charles spaniel, the Cavalier was bred with pug-type dogs to produce a domed head and short snout.

Trainability   Eager to please

Brussels Griffon

Factfile

Personality	Loyal, alert, curious
Height	7 to 10 in.
Weight	7 to 12 lb.
Exercise	15 to 30 minutes
Grooming	2 to 3 times a week
Life span	12 to 15 years

History While its forebears were the wire-haired terrier ratters of Belgium stables, the modern breed comes from the affenpinscher, pug and English toy spaniel.

Fact This "grumpy-faced" bearded dog is fairly rare today, as they are difficult to breed, and after WW II were almost extinct in their native Belgium.

Trainability	Agreeable

54

Pekingese

Factfile

Personality	Affectionate, devoted, regal
Height	6 to 9 in.
Weight	7 to 14 lb.
Exercise	30 minutes
Grooming	Daily
Life span	14 to 18 years

History The breed began in ancient China. Only the imperial family could own them, and common people had to bow down to the Pekingese!

Fact Pekingese come in 10 colors, with three different types of markings. Their fur can get very long, so a regular trim is very important.

Trainability — Stubborn

Pug

Dogs

Toy dog

Factfile

Personality	Charming, mischievous, loving
Height	10 to 14 in.
Weight	13 to 20 lb.
Exercise	20 minutes, twice a day
Grooming	Weekly
Life span	12 to 15 years

History Centuries old, this Asian breed, with its Pekingese and shih tzu heritage, was intended to be a royal pet. Some even had their own palaces and guards.

Fact Its wrinkly face may be full of character, but its short, flat nose causes breathing problems. The ideal pug tail has a tight, double upward curl.

Trainability Stubborn

Havanese

Factfile

Personality	Intelligent, outgoing, happy
Height	8.5 to 11.5 in.
Weight	8 to 13 lb.
Exercise	20 to 40 minutes, plus games
Grooming	2 to 3 times a week
Life span	14 to 16 years

History Cuba's national dog, this bichon-similar breed first came from the Mediterranean. Traders would curry favor by gifting them to Cuban merchants.

Fact Small, clever Havanese have been trained to be service, therapy, assistance and tracking dogs. They can also detect mold and termites.

Trainability	Easy to train

German Shepherd

Factfile

Personality	Confident, courageous, smart
Height	22 to 26 in.
Weight	48 to 88 lb.
Exercise	At least 2 hours
Grooming	2 to 3 times a week
Life span	9 to 13 years

History The first German shepherd appeared in 1899. Named Horand, he was grandfather to Beowulf, to whom all modern German shepherds are genetically linked.

Fact These are obedient working dogs that thrive on being challenged. One German shepherd female learned 100 tricks by her first birthday!

Trainability   Eager to please

Australian Shepherd

Factfile

Personality	Smart, work oriented, exuberant
Height	18 to 23 in.
Weight	40 to 65 lb.
Exercise	Vigorous 1 hour, plus games
Grooming	Weekly
Life span	12 to 15 years

History A European herding dog was crossed with collies and shepherds to create the breed. They first appeared in Australia in the 1800s.

Fact Australian Shepherds were refined in California, where they herded livestock, performed in rodeos, and became a symbol of the American West.

Trainability	Easy to train

Miniature American Shepherd

Factfile

Personality	Good-natured, intelligent, devoted
Height	13 to 18 in.
Weight	17 to 40 lb.
Exercise	Vigorous 1 hour, plus games
Grooming	Weekly
Life span	12 to 16 years

History The breed first appeared in the 1960s in California, when small Australian shepherds were bred down to produce even smaller offspring.

Fact These highly intelligent dogs do well in dog sports like agility, herding, nose work and obedience. If bored, they may bark to let everyone know.

Trainability   **Eager to please**

Collie

Factfile

Personality	Devoted, graceful, proud
Height	22 to 26 in.
Weight	50 to 75 lb.
Exercise	At least 2 hours, plus games
Grooming	2 to 3 times a week
Life span	12 to 14 years

History Roman herding dogs appeared in Scotland 2,000 years ago, and over the centuries were crossed with local breeds to create the modern collie.

Fact Eric Knight's novel *Lassie Come-Home* made the collie a celebrity in print. Pal played the first onscreen Lassie, then his offspring took over the role.

Trainability	**Easy to train**

61

Bearded Collie

Factfile

Personality	Smart, bouncy, charismatic
Height	20 to 22 in.
Weight	40 to 59 lb.
Exercise	1 to 2 hours, plus games
Grooming	Daily
Life span	12 to 14 years

History The bearded collie is descended from lowland Polish sheepdogs swapped by a Polish trader for a few Scottish sheep in the 1500s.

Fact Even tempered and cheerful, this is not a breed to be underestimated – it will turn training into a game of its own choosing.

Trainability	Independent

Border Collie

Factfile

Personality	Affectionate, smart, energetic
Height	18 to 22 in.
Weight	26 to 55 lb.
Exercise	At least 2 hours, plus games
Grooming	2 to 3 times a week
Life span	12 to 15 years

History The border collie breed is likely a cross between large Roman herding dogs and the smaller spitz-type the Vikings brought to Britain.

Fact Named the "Smartest Dog in the World," border collie Chaser learned the names of 1,022 objects and understood complex sentences.

Trainability	Eager to please

Belgian Tervuren

Factfile

Personality	Courageous, alert, intelligent
Height	22 to 26 in.
Weight	60 to 75 lb.
Exercise	1 hour, plus games
Grooming	Twice a week
Life span	12 to 14 years

History One of four Belgian herding breeds, little is known of the Tervuren's history. Its long coat may be any color but black.

Fact With strong herding and chase instincts, they will run after joggers, cyclists and cars, so should be kept safe on the leash and in fenced yards.

Trainability — Easy to train

Belgian Malinois

Factfile

Personality	Confident, smart, hardworking
Height	22 to 26 in.
Weight	37 to 80 lb.
Exercise	At least 90 minutes
Grooming	Weekly; daily when shedding
Life span	14 to 16 years

History Named for their home city, Malines, Belgium, these short-haired, fawn-colored dogs are always ready for work or exercise.

Fact Belgian Malinois are often used by the military. Some have even been trained for tandem parachute jumps, strapped to their handlers.

Trainability	Easy to train

Puli

Factfile

Personality	Loyal, smart, homebody
Height	16 to 17 in.
Weight	25 to 35 lb.
Exercise	At least 40 minutes
Grooming	Don't brush; separate cords as needed
Life span	10 to 15 years

History A native Asian breed, the puli ended up in Hungary 1,000 years ago. They are quick and agile, ideal for sheepdogs.

Fact The puli earned its "push-me, pull-me" nickname because its mop-like tail curls back over its body, making it hard to tell which end is which.

Trainability — **Independent**

Bouvier des Flandres

Factfile

Personality	Affectionate, courageous, strong willed
Height	23 to 35 in.
Weight	59 to 90 lb.
Exercise	At least 40 minutes
Grooming	2 to 3 times a week
Life span	10 to 12 years

History They have been used by Belgian farmers as herders ("bouvier" means cowherd), watchdogs and cart pullers, but not much is known of the breed's history.

Fact The Bouvier's curly double coat traps everything from leaves and dirt to twigs and water, so they must be cleaned (and dried off!) often.

Trainability	Agreeable

Briard

Factfile

Personality	Confident, smart, faithful
Height	22 to 27 in.
Weight	58 to 100 lb.
Exercise	At least 40 minutes
Grooming	Daily
Life span	12 years

History Named for the French cheese region of Brie, the briard continues to herd and protect flocks. In the 1700s they were crossed with beauceron and barbet.

Fact President Thomas Jefferson had the first US briard, Buzzy. He imported many, using them to guard his merino flocks at Monticello.

Trainability	**Independent**

Old English Sheepdog

Factfile

Personality	Adaptable, gentle, smart, clownish
Height	21 in. min.
Weight	60 to 90 lb.
Exercise	20 to 40 minutes
Grooming	2 to 3 times a week
Life span	10 to 12 years

History This large breed was first developed in the UK in the 1700s, to drive livestock long distances to market and protect herds from wolves.

Fact In the UK in the 1800s, working dogs with tails were taxed, so Old English sheepdog tails were docked to avoid having to pay.

Trainability	Independent

Shetland Sheepdog

Factfile

Personality	Playful, energetic, intelligent
Height	13 to 16 in.
Weight	15 to 26 lb.
Exercise	At least 1 hour
Grooming	2 to 3 times a week
Life span	12 to 14 years

History A descendant of small Scottish collies, King Charles spaniels and rough collies, the Sheltie's vigor reflected the harshness of its native Shetland Islands.

Fact Ranked as the sixth most intelligent breed by the American Kennel Club, today's Shetland is not a working dog and is rare on the Shetlands.

Trainability   Eager to please

Cardigan Welsh Corgi

Factfile

Personality	Affectionate, loyal, smart
Height	10 to 13 in.
Weight	25 to 38 lb.
Exercise	20 to 40 minutes
Grooming	Twice a week
Life span	12 to 15 years

History The Cardigan is one of the UK's oldest herding breeds. It arrived in Wales 3,000 years ago and shares some ancestry with the Dachshund.

Fact This "yard-long dog" was purposely bred to be low to the ground – able to avoid being kicked by cattle.

Trainability	Agreeable

71

Pembroke Welsh Corgi

Factfile

Personality	Affectionate, smart, alert
Height	10 to 12 in.
Weight	24 to 31 lb.
Exercise	20 to 40 minutes
Grooming	Weekly
Life span	12 to 14 years

History Dogs brought to Wales in 1107 by Flemish weavers were the foundation of this tailless breed, with several other breeds also contributing to its ancestry.

Fact Welsh legend has it that fairies and elves used Pembrokes to pull fairy carts. Willow, the last of Queen Elizabeth II's five corgis, died in 2018.

Trainability	Easy to train

Norwegian Buhund

Factfile

Personality	Confident, clever, perceptive
Height	16 to 18.5 in.
Weight	25 to 40 lb.
Exercise	1 hour, twice a day
Grooming	Three times a week; daily when shedding
Life span	12 to 15 years

History Buhund ("bu" means farm or homestead) date back to 900 CE. They traveled with the Vikings and were the breed stock for the modern buhund.

Fact When Vikings died, valuable possessions were buried with them. These included buhund that would herd and protect them in the next life.

Trainability　　　　　**Easy to train**

Basenji

Factfile

Personality	Independent, smart, poised
Height	16 to 17 in.
Weight	21 to 24 lb.
Exercise	40 to 60 minutes
Grooming	Twice a week
Life span	13 to 14 years

History This ancient bush dog breed's instinct to run and chase comes from its Egyptian street dog and Congolese hunting dog ancestry.

Fact The Basenji has highly developed sight and sense of smell, but cannot bark – it yodels! To locate it in forests, bells were fitted around its neck.

Trainability	Independent

74

Ibizan Hound

Factfile

Personality	Family oriented, even tempered, intelligent
Height	22 to 27.5 in.
Weight	40 to 50 lb.
Exercise	30 minutes, plus yard play
Grooming	At least once a week
Life span	11 to 14 years

History This 5,000-year-old breed may be seen in Egyptian tomb art and hieroglyphs. When Ibiza, Spain, became its home, it hunted rabbits for the table.

Fact Although it is also fast, it's the Ibizan's agility that is astounding. It can leap tall fences from a standing start, and climb and unlock gates.

Trainability	Independent

Norwegian Elkhound

Factfile

Personality	Friendly, confident, dependable
Height	18 to 21 in.
Weight	40 to 60 lb.
Exercise	Vigorous 60 minutes
Grooming	Weekly
Life span	12 to 15 years

History The Norwegian elkhound's ancestors go back 6,000 years to hunting swamp dogs. It is a spitz-type dog, like the Akita, malamute and Samoyed.

Fact When it located a moose the elkhound barked softly to alert the hunter, then circled the moose, leaping at it until the hunter was close.

Trainability	Agreeable

Afghan Hound

Factfile

Personality	Aloof, strong willed, clownish
Height	24 to 27 in.
Weight	50 to 60 lb.
Exercise	At least 2 hours
Grooming	Daily
Life span	12 to 18 years

History An Asian hunting dog with acute sight and great stamina and agility, this ancient breed has much in common with the gazelle-chasing saluki.

Fact In Korea in 2005, a cell from an Afghan was cloned to produce the world's first canine clone. It was named Snuppy, for Seoul National University Puppy.

Trainability	Stubborn

Greyhound

Factfile

Personality	Gentle, athletic, noble
Height	27 to 30 in.
Weight	60 to 70 lb.
Exercise	At least 1 hour
Grooming	Weekly; check skin daily
Life span	10 to 13 years

History Instantly recognizable, the greyhound has remained unchanged since 3000 BCE. It has been a hunter, racer and companion to royalty and commoners alike.

Fact Greyhounds can run up to 45 mph (the average for other breeds is 20 mph). They also like to relax, earning their "45-mph couch potato" nickname.

Trainability	Independent

Whippet

Factfile

Personality	Affectionate, playful, calm
Height	17 to 20 in.
Weight	20 to 42 lb.
Exercise	At least 1 hour
Grooming	Weekly; check skin daily
Life span	12 to 15 years

History The whippet's history is unclear – terrier and greyhound cross or simply miniature greyhound. They first hunted rabbit for the table and raced for sport.

Fact Whippets have little body fat and a short coat, so lose body heat very quickly. When running, their feet are off the ground twice per stride.

Trainability   **Independent**

Irish Wolfhound

Factfile

Personality	Courageous, dignified, calm
Height	32 to 35 in.
Weight	115 to 180 lb.
Exercise	At least 40 minutes
Grooming	Weekly
Life span	6 to 10 years

History Irish wolfhounds may have come to Ireland in 7000 BCE as war or hunting dogs. Modern wolfhounds may have borzoi, Great Dane, deerhound and mastiff ancestry.

Fact The tallest breed, these "gentle when stroked, fierce when provoked" giants can stand 7 feet tall on their hind legs.

Trainability	**Independent**

Factfile

Personality	Affectionate, loyal, regal
Height	26 in. min.
Weight	60 to 105 lb.
Exercise	1 to 2 hours, plus yard play
Grooming	Weekly
Life span	9 to 14 years

History Originating in Russia in the 1600s, these strong, graceful sight hounds hunted wolves for the aristocracy, holding their prey until hunters arrived.

Fact Borzoi rarely bark and are so light on their feet it's hard to hear them coming. Their desire to run is strong, so sturdy leashes and fences are needed.

Trainability **Independent**

Saluki

Factfile

Personality	Gentle, dignified, affectionate
Height	23 to 28 in.
Weight	35 to 65 lb.
Exercise	Vigorous 40 minutes, plus yard play
Grooming	Weekly; feathering often
Life span	10 to 17 years

History Saluki once hunted gazelle and fast game in deserts. Though domesticated for 5,000 years, their genetic similarity to wolves is among the highest.

Fact This "royal dog" was so valued by ancient Egyptians it would be mummified at death. Today, the breed is well known to be finicky about food.

Trainability	Independent

Basset Hound

Factfile

Personality	Charming, patient, undemanding
Height	11 to 15 in.
Weight	40 to 60 lb.
Exercise	Up to 1 hour
Grooming	Twice a week
Life span	12 to 13 years

History Developed in the 1500s by French friars and later refined in the UK, the basset tracked game with its nose low ("bas") to the ground.

Fact With over 220 million receptors, the basset hound's scenting ability may be aided by its distinctive features, which trap smells near its nasal cavities.

Trainability	Independent

Petit Basset Griffon Vendéen

Factfile

Personality	Alert, happy, vivacious
Height	13 to 15 in.
Weight	25 to 40 lb.
Exercise	30 minutes, twice a day
Grooming	Daily
Life span	14 to 16 years

History This scent hound was used to track guinea fowl, rabbits and hare over the rough terrain of France's Vendéen region. It is one of four griffon Vendéens.

Fact A scruffy, wirehaired hound nicknamed the "happy dog," it will bark at a burglar but then lick them in welcome.

Trainability	Independent

Grand Basset Griffon Vendéen

Factfile

Personality	Alert, happy, vivacious
Height	15 to 18 in.
Weight	40 to 44 lb.
Exercise	At least 2 hours
Grooming	Daily
Life span	13 to 15 years

History Petit and grands were bred from the same mix of hounds and rough-coated dogs, but since the 1970s have been classed as separate breeds.

Fact Grands are bigger, with longer snouts than petits, and their legs are straight while the petits' can be kinked. Grands also come in more colors.

Trainability	Independent

Beagle

Factfile

Personality	Friendly, curious, smart
Height	13 to 16 in.
Weight	22 to 35 lb.
Exercise	30 to 60 minutes, twice or three times a day
Grooming	Weekly
Life span	10 to 15 years

History Crossing southern hounds and north country beagles resulted in four types of beagle in the 1800s. Today, there is only one standard.

Fact Charles M. Shultz's comic strip, *Peanuts*, features Snoopy, the world's most famous beagle. The always dreaming but silent Snoopy first appeared in 1950.

Trainability	Stubborn

Otterhound

Factfile

Personality	Amlable, boisterous, devoted
Height	24 to 28 in.
Weight	66 to 120 lb.
Exercise	At least 30 minutes, twice a day, plus swimming
Grooming	Weekly
Life span	10 to 13 years

History Otterhound heritage most likely includes griffon Vendéen, de Bresse and Nivernais. From the 1700s to 1978 it hunted otters depleting UK fish stocks.

Fact With only 800 in the world, this highly endangered breed is rarer than a giant panda or white rhino. Breeding fell when otter hunting was banned in the UK.

Trainability	Stubborn

Bloodhound

Factfile

Personality   Friendly, independent, inquisitive
Height   23 to 27 in.
Weight   80 to 110 lb.
Exercise   At least 2 hours
Grooming   Weekly
Life span   10 to 12 years

History The breed probably came from the same friary that created the basset. They could scent and find prey, especially bleeding prey, and thieves!

Fact Bloodhounds have 300 million scent receptors. One sleuthhound (the name in the 1600s) scented for seven miles and tracked its quarry – a man – to an upstairs room.

Trainability	Independent

Dachshund

Factfile

Personality	Curious, lively, attention loving
Height	Standard 8 to 9 in. / Miniature 5 to 6 in.
Weight	Standard 16 to 32 lb. / Miniature 11 lb. max.
Exercise	1 hour (adult dog only)
Grooming	Weekly
Life span	12 to 16 years

History With terrier and hound ancestry, this 400-year-old German breed, with its long, low-slung body, was ideal for chasing badgers ("dachs") from tunnels.

Fact "Wiener dogs" are fearless, with loud barks, making them excellent watchdogs. One study ranked them the most aggressive dog breed.

Trainability   **Agreeable**

Rhodesian Ridgeback

Factfile

Personality	Affectionate, dignified, even tempered
Height	24 to 27 in.
Weight	65 to 90 lb.
Exercise	At least 2 hours
Grooming	Weekly
Life span	10 to 12 years

History This South African breed was a cross between native Khoikhoi dogs and European greyhounds and terriers. They hunt by sight and scent.

Fact Named for the ridge of hair on its spine that grows opposite the rest, ridgebacks could track a lion and keep it at bay until hunters arrived.

Trainability   Independent

Black and Tan Coonhound

Factfile

Personality	Easygoing, bright, brave
Height	23 to 27 in.
Weight	50 to 75 lb.
Exercise	At least 40 minutes
Grooming	Weekly
Life span	10 to 12 years

History One of six coonhound breeds, it was developed – a mix of English foxhound and bloodhound – by early US settlers to hunt raccoons.

Fact A black-and-tan will emit a bark that is different than its "chasing" bark to alert hunters that a raccoon has been treed.

Trainability	Independent

Miniature Schnauzer

Factfile

Personality	Friendly, smart, obedient
Height	12 to 14 in.
Weight	11 to 20 lb.
Exercise	At least 30 minutes
Grooming	Weekly
Life span	12 to 15 years

History This dog stays true to schnauzer character and type, but was most likely a cross of standard schnauzer, affenpinscher and other small breeds.

Fact Partnered with a German shepherd to protect the farm, the miniature would bark at the slightest noise to alert the "muscle" dog to action.

Trainability   Eager to please

Airedale Terrier

Factfile

Personality	Friendly, clever, courageous
Height	22 to 24 in.
Weight	55 to 77 lb.
Exercise	Vigorous 45 minutes
Grooming	Twice a week
Life span	11 to 14 years

History Initially bred in Airedale, UK, in the 1800s, the modern Airedale has otterhound and Irish and bull terrier heritage. It is the largest of all the terriers.

Fact In 1918, a heroic Airedale named Jack was shot twice delivering a British battalion's request for help. He died, but the soldiers were saved.

Trainability	Eager to please

Border Terrier

Factfile

Personality	Affectionate, happy, plucky
Height	11 to 16 in.
Weight	11 to 16 lb.
Exercise	1 to 2 hours
Grooming	Weekly
Life span	12 to 15 years

History On hill country farms on the Scotland-England border, these terriers kept foxes under control. It shares ancestors with Bedlington and Dandie Dinmont terriers.

Fact These feisty, small terriers could chase a fox from its lair, or trap it underground, barking to indicate its location to hunters on horseback.

Trainability	Easy to train

Bull Terrier

Factfile

Personality	Playful, charming, mischievous
Height	18 to 22 in.
Weight	45 to 65 lb.
Exercise	1 hour
Grooming	Weekly
Life span	12 to 15 years

History The first bull terriers appeared in 1862. A cross of bulldog, English white terrier (extinct) and Dalmatian, those with white coats are the most popular.

Fact Although its reputation as a fierce fighter is well deserved, bull terriers also make affectionate pets and perform well as show dogs.

Trainability	Independent

Cairn Terrier

Factfile

Personality	Alert, cheerful, busy
Height	9 to 10 in.
Weight	13 to 14 lb.
Exercise	Vigorous 30 minutes
Grooming	Weekly
Life span	12 to 15 years

History Pest controllers par excellence since the 1500s, cairns won't stop until their work is done. They come from the Scottish Highlands and islands.

Fact The cairn's instinct is to chase, so it will take off after cats, squirrels and other dogs unless leashed, and won't always come when called.

Trainability

Irish Terrier

Factfile

Personality	Bold, dashing, sensitive
Height	18 to 19 in.
Weight	24 to 33 lb.
Exercise	30 minutes, three times a day
Grooming	Weekly
Life span	13 to 15 years

History Descended from UK black-and-tan terriers – and maybe Irish wolfhounds – the "farmer's friend" is long-legged and a natural vermin killer.

Fact The breed standard describes the Irish as "racy, red and rectangular." Their bright-red or golden-red coat may display a white patch on the chest.

Trainability	Agreeable

97

Wire Fox Terrier

Factfile

Personality	Confident, alert, gregarious
Height	14 to 15.5 in.
Weight	15 to 19 lb.
Exercise	30 to 40 minutes
Grooming	Weekly
Life span	12 to 15 years

History Established in the late 1700s, most likely from white Old English terrier and beagle or bull terrier, the goal was a dog to flush foxes from their dens.

Fact Wire fox terriers are the top "Best in Show" breed. Dogs have won the US Westminster Kennel Club Show 14 times and UK Crufts three times!

Trainability   **Agreeable**

Smooth Fox Terrier

Factfile

Personality	Friendly, independent, amusing
Height	14 to 15.5 in.
Weight	15 to 19 lb.
Exercise	30 to 40 minutes
Grooming	Weekly
Life span	12 to 15 years

History Smooth fox terriers rode in a horse's saddlebags to be released when the fox went to ground. They were essential to the hunt.

Fact The only differences between the smooth and wire fox terrier are coat texture, markings and head shape. The smooth fox has a longer head.

Trainability	Agreeable

Scottish Terrier

Factfile

Personality	Confident, independent, spirited
Height	10 to 11 in.
Weight	18 to 22 lb.
Exercise	30 minutes
Grooming	2 to 3 times a week
Life span	12 to 15 years

History Scottish terriers were developed to hunt rats, badgers and foxes in the Scottish Highlands. Body "feathers" conceal its sturdy legs.

Fact Loyal and feisty, Scotties have been "first dog" companions to three presidents: Franklin D. Roosevelt, Dwight D. Eisenhower and George W. Bush.

Trainability	Independent

Soft-coated Wheaten Terrier

Factfile

Personality	Friendly, happy, devoted
Height	17 to 19 in.
Weight	30 to 40 lb.
Exercise	1 hour
Grooming	2 to 3 times a week
Life span	10 to 15 years

History With ancestry that includes Kerry blue terrier and Irish terrier, this "poor man's dog" herded and guarded livestock, and hunted and killed vermin.

Fact Wheaten puppies are born with a dark-brown coat which lightens during their first two years to the color of grains of wheat.

Trainability	Independent

Bedlington Terrier

Factfile

Personality	Loyal, charming, frisky
Height	15 to 17.5 in.
Weight	17 to 23 lb.
Exercise	40 minutes
Grooming	Daily
Life span	12 to 16 years

History Bedlingtons may look soft and fluffy, but these were working dogs, catching rats down mines and swimming, with a "pit fighter" reputation.

Fact Judges at dog shows always look for the topknot (the tuft of longer hair on the top of the dog's head) to be a lighter shade than the body color.

Trainability	Agreeable

Staffordshire Bull Terrier

Factfile

Personality	Clever, brave, tenacious
Height	14 to 16 in.
Weight	24 to 38 lb.
Exercise	1 to 2 hours
Grooming	Twice a week
Life span	9 to 16 years

History This bulldog and small terrier cross has a reputation earned through fighting, but also one as a working dog and devoted companion.

Fact Staffies thrive on mental and physical challenges like agility and flyball. In Australia, it is the second most popular breed; in the UK, it's the third.

Trainability   Stubborn

103

West Highland White Terrier

Factfile

Personality	Loyal, happy, entertaining
Height	10 to 11 in.
Weight	15 to 20 lb.
Exercise	1 hour
Grooming	Daily
Life span	13 to 15 years

History This vermin hunter is closely related to Scottish and cairn terriers, but was developed for its white coat – easy to see in fields during the hunt.

Fact Though it is decades since the Westie has had to earn its keep, it retains its instincts and will go to earth, chasing rodents and flushing moles from the garden.

Trainability   Stubborn

Parson Russell Terrier

Factfile

Personality	Friendly, clever, determined
Height	13 to 14 in.
Weight	13 to 17 lb.
Exercise	1 to 2 hours
Grooming	Weekly
Life span	13 to 15 years

History These terriers are known for their ability to dig foxes from dens. Though very similar to the Jack Russell, the smaller Parson might have Welsh corgi heritage.

Fact In 1818, Reverend John Russell bought a terrier called Trump from a milkman. Trump became the foundation for this breed that could run with foxhounds.

Trainability	Agreeable

Factfile

Personality	Loyal, alert, calm
Height	Toy 10 to 14 in. / Mini 14 to 18 in. / Standard 18 to 23 in.
Weight	Toy 10 to 15 lb. / Mini 15 to 30 lb. / Standard 30 to 55 lb.
Exercise	30 minutes
Grooming	Wash feet weekly
Life span	12 to 15 years

History The Xolo is an ancient, naturally evolved breed. Brought to Mexico from Asia, it was used by Aztecs as a bed warmer and as a sacrifice.

Fact Also known as the Mexican hairless dog, Xolos have tough, close-fitting skin, with tufts of hair on points. Aztecs believed the Xolo had healing powers.

Trainability	**Agreeable**

Factfile

Personality	Willful, aloof, quiet
Height	18 to 22 in.
Weight	39 to 64 lb.
Exercise	15 minutes, four times a day
Grooming	Weekly
Life span	8 to 15 years

History Sharing chow chow ancestry, these were hunting and fighting dogs. Their wrinkled, loose skin and bristly coat minimized a rival's ability to grip.

Fact Shar-pei means "harsh sandy coat." They may have a blue-black or lavender colored tongue, but Chinese folklore says black wards off evil spirits.

Trainability	Stubborn

Chow Chow

Factfile

Personality	Aloof, clever, serious
Height	17 to 20 in.
Weight	45 to 70 lb.
Exercise	15 minutes, three times a day
Grooming	2 to 3 times a week
Life span	8 to 12 years

History The most ancient of all Chinese breeds, one emperor may have kept as many as 5,000 chows in his kennel. They could pull sleds, hunt and guard livestock.

Fact Chows are born with pink tongues that turn blue-black after 8 to 10 weeks. The statues outside Buddhist temples may be modeled on this breed.

Trainability	Stubborn

Factfile

Personality	Friendly, lively, outgoing
Height	16 to 19 in.
Weight	35 to 45 lb.
Exercise	1 hour
Grooming	Daily
Life span	12 to 15 years

History This spitz-type dog was a watchdog on Dutch barges in the 17th and 18th centuries, but fell out of favor for years after becoming a symbol of a defeated political party.

Fact Dark lines that run from ears to eyes, and circles around the eyes make it look like keeshonden are wearing glasses, but the marks are a breed standard.

Trainability | **Easy to train**

Factfile

Personality	Confident, alert, curious
Height	10 to 13 in.
Weight	12 to 16 lb.
Exercise	40 minutes, plus yard play
Grooming	Weekly
Life span	12 to 16 years

History Schipperke – "little captain" in Flemish – were dockyard and barge vermin catchers. First known in the 1400s, they are sheepdog descendants.

Fact Schipperke are wary of strangers and not afraid to bark (a lot!), so make excellent watchdogs, and remain great boat dogs.

Trainability   **Independent**

Factfile

Personality	Playful, perky, smart
Height	Toy 9 to 12 in. / Mini 12 to 15 in. / Standard 15 to 19 in.
Weight	Toy 6 to 10 lb. / Mini 10 to 20 lb. / Standard 20 to 35 lb.
Exercise	40 minutes, plus yard play
Grooming	2 to 3 times a week
Life span	13 to 15 years

History A spitz-type dog first bred in the US in the 1800s by German immigrants to be a watchdog, their loud bark makes up for their lack of aggression.

Fact Eskimos earn top scores in obedience trials. This, and their eagerness to learn tricks, made them popular performers in traveling circuses.

Trainability   **Eager to please**

Shiba Inu

Factfile

Personality	Alert, active, intelligent
Height	13 to 17 in.
Weight	16 to 20 lb.
Exercise	45 minutes, every two days
Grooming	Weekly
Life span	13 to 16 years

History This Japanese breed has been around for over 2,000 years. It was used to hunt and would flush small game and birds from the brush wood ("shiba").

Fact Shiba Inu are one of Japan's national treasures. In 1945 just three remained and only a breeding program guaranteed the breed's survival.

Trainability	Independent

Factfile

Personality	Dignified, smart, outgoing
Height	19 to 23 in.
Weight	45 to 77 lb.
Exercise	2 hours
Grooming	Weekly
Life span	11 to 13 years

History Its origins are unclear, but in the 1800s in central Europe it would run beside carriages to prevent other dogs or animals from spooking the horses.

Fact Dalmatian puppies are born with a white coat – the spots develop 2 to 3 weeks later. Often portrayed as fire station mascots, deafness is common in the breed.

Trainability **Agreeable**

Factfile

Personality	Active, proud, intelligent
Height	15 to 24 in.
Weight	45 to 70 lb.
Exercise	30 minutes, twice a day, plus occasional swim
Grooming	3 times a week
Life span	12 to 15 years

History One of the world's oldest purebreds, the standard became a distinct breed in France but originated in Germany. As a hunter, it retrieved from water.

Fact To attract audiences to the circus, poodles were trimmed with pom-poms of fur on their head, legs and tail – a style reminiscent of a clown outfit.

Trainability	Eager to please

Factfile

Personality	Active, proud, intelligent
Height	10 to 15 in.
Weight	15 to 17 lb.
Exercise	20 minutes, three times a day
Grooming	Daily
Life span	14 to 17 years

History Miniatures appeared in the 1400s after ever-smaller standards were bred. Prized as truffle hunters, their tiny paws left truffles undamaged.

Fact Poodles shed little and can be groomed frequently, so may be hypoallergenic, though there is no guarantee they are completely allergen free.

Trainability   **Eager to please**

Bichon Frise

Factfile

Personality	Playful, curious, even tempered
Height	10 to 15 in.
Weight	12 to 22 lb.
Exercise	30 minutes
Grooming	Daily
Life span	13 to 17 years

History Bichon frise ancestors were water spaniels and standard poodles from the 1300s. They were companions to sailors and aristocrats.

Fact Its origins might suggest a water dog, but bichons are much happier as lap dogs and prefer to stay well away from water.

Trainability   Agreeable

Factfile

Personality	Adaptable, playful, smart
Height	11 to 13 in.
Weight	16 to 28 lb.
Exercise	10 to 15 minutes, twice a day
Grooming	Weekly
Life span	10 to 12 years

History Originating from the toy English bulldog, they once warmed the laps of lace makers. When lace making was relocated to France in the 1800s, Frenchies went too.

Fact The most distinctive features of the breed are the "bat-like" ears (rose shaped in the UK) and creased, pudgy face with squashed nose.

Trainability	**Agreeable**

Bulldog

Factfile

Personality	Friendly, courageous, calm
Height	10 to 15 in.
Weight	40 to 55 lb.
Exercise	10 to 15 minutes, twice a day
Grooming	Weekly; clean face daily
Life span	8 to 10 years

History Bulldogs were bred over 800 years ago for bull baiting. In this gruesome "sport," a tethered bull fought a pack of dogs in front of spectators.

Fact This breed is brachycephalic, a condition caused by its short snout which makes breathing difficult and snoring and snorting likely.

Trainability	Agreeable

Lhasa Apso

Factfile

Personality	Confident, smart, comical
Height	9 to 11 in.
Weight	11 to 16 lb.
Exercise	25 minutes, twice a day
Grooming	Daily
Life span	12 to 15 years

History The Lhasa apso was bred centuries ago as a watchdog for Buddhist monks in Tibet. The aim was a dog that closely resembled a lion in color and shape.

Fact It was hard to find this long-haired breed outside of Tibet until 1933, when the Dalai Lama gifted a pair of dogs to an American dignitary.

Trainability	**Independent**

Tibetan Spaniel

Factfile

Personality	Playful, bright, self-confident
Height	9 to 10 in.
Weight	9 to 15 lb.
Exercise	20 to 40 minutes
Grooming	Daily
Life span	12 to 15 years

History Tibetan villagers saved the smallest, most prized Tibetans for the monks. These keen-sighted dogs were watchdogs and may have turned prayer wheels.

Fact The much-valued Tibetan was never sold, only given as a gift. It is believed that the Chinese crossed it with their own pugs to produce the Pekingese.

Trainability   **Agreeable**

Boston Terrier

Factfile

Personality	Friendly, bright, amusing
Height	15 to 17 in.
Weight	12 to 25 lb.
Exercise	At least 40 minutes, plus games
Grooming	Weekly
Life span	11 to 15 years

History Appearing in 1869, the US's first purebred breed is a cross between English bulldogs and English terriers. It is the state dog of Massachusetts.

Fact Boston terrier Sgt. Stubby served in WW I with US soldiers. He warned them of mustard attacks and comforted wounded soldiers.

Trainability   **Eager to please**

121

Tibetan Terrier

Factfile

Personality	Affectionate, sensitive, mischievous, smart
Height	13 to 17 in.
Weight	17 to 30 lb.
Exercise	30 minutes, twice a day
Grooming	2 to 3 times a week
Life span	15 to 17 years

History The "holy dogs of Tibet" were believed to be lucky omens by the monks who bred them. They also worked, bringing items up the mountain.

Fact Despite its name, the Tibetan is not a terrier. The name comes from its size and liveliness. Its long eyelashes guarantee that long hair stays out of its eyes.

Trainability   Independent

Cockapoo

Factfile

Personality	Happy, friendly, affectionate
Height	10 to 15 in.
Weight	12 to 24 lb.
Exercise	30 minutes twice a day, plus yard play
Grooming	Twice a week
Life span	14 to 18 years

History As the name indicates, this is a cocker spaniel and poodle cross. It first appeared in the US in the 1950s. In some countries, it is called a "spoodle."

Fact The goal with this breed was to create the perfect family pet. Its cheerfulness and sociability also make it an excellent therapy dog.

Trainability	Easy to train

123

Standard Labradoodle

Factfile

Personality	Playful, affectionate, intelligent
Height	21 to 24 in.
Weight	50 to 65 lb.
Exercise	30 to 60 minutes
Grooming	Twice a week
Life span	12 to 15 years

History Labrador retriever and poodle cross, the labradoodle was created in Australia in 1988 to be low shedding and suitable for allergy sufferers.

Fact These gentle, well-behaved dogs form bonds quickly and are often used as guide dogs. Smaller versions are the medium and miniature.

Trainability   **Easy to train**

Standard Goldendoodle

Factfile

Personality	Friendly, intelligent, outgoing
Height	20 to 25 in.
Weight	50 to 70 lb.
Exercise	30 minutes, three times a day
Grooming	Daily
Life span	10 to 15 years

History This golden retriever and poodle cross first appeared in the 1990s. Breeders aimed to create an active family pet that was very low shedding.

Fact If left to its own devices, the golden retriever in the breed comes out in a yard full of holes! There are also miniature and tiny (toy) goldendoodles.

Trainability   **Easy to train**

Glossary

Agility A canine sport where a handler guides his or her dog around an obstacle course.

Beard Thick, coarse hair around the lower face.

Breed Dogs that share common genes and similar appearance.

Companion Dog that wants to spend time with its owner.

Corded Coat of naturally formed, dreadlock-like long hair.

Crossbreed To mate dogs of different breeds together.

Docile Quiet, not aggressive, and easily controlled.

Domesticated An animal brought under human control.

Double coat An insulating undercoat with a weatherproof or weather resistant top layer.

Extinct An animal without any living specimens.

Feathering Fringes of hair on ears, tummy, back of legs or underside of tail.

Flyball A canine race where dogs run, release, and catch balls.

Flush In hunting, to drive a game bird or animal from its cover and into the open.

Game Wild animals, often birds, hunted for sport or food.

Gun dog A hunting or sporting dog that can flush, point and/or retrieve game.

Herding Moving or gathering together a group of farm animals.

Insulated Dog's fur that stops heat escaping the body.

Livestock Animals, like cows or sheep, that are kept on a farm.

Mask A dark coloration across a dog's upper face.

Muzzle The projecting parts – nose and mouth – of a dog's face.

Obedient A dog that will follow commands and instructions.

Pack A group of dogs that live or hunt together.

Particolor Coat with patches in different colors.

Pedigree A dog's recorded ancestry or bloodline.

Pet A domestic or tamed animal that is kept and cared for as a companion, not for work.

Point In hunting, when a dog points its snout toward the prey.

Points These are the dog's head, face, ears, tail and legs.

Purebred A dog with a defined pedigree.

Ratter A dog with natural instincts (though sometimes trained) to catch rats and other small rodents.

Retrieve In hunting, when a dog locates felled game, especially birds, and carries it in its mouth to the hunter without further damaging the prey.

Scent Odor trail of an animal or human that a dog can track.

Setter In hunting, a dog that stands or crouches motionless when it locates game.

Selective breeding Choosing dog types to breed based on their characteristics, with the aim of passing the desirable features on to the next generation.

Snout See Muzzle

Spitz Dog type that has thick, long fur (often white) and pointed ears and muzzle.

Temperament A dog's personality and character.

Middle Ages A period in European history between 500 and 1500 CE.

Track A natural ability or trained technique by which a dog can locate objects, animals or humans by their scent.

Vermin Animals, like rats, wolves and raccoons, that ravage crops and food stores, carry disease or attack farm animals.

Water dog A retriever type of dog bred to flush game from the water and to bring felled game back to the hunter.

Webbed paws A thin membrane of skin between the toes that allows a dog to paddle though water with efficiency.

Index